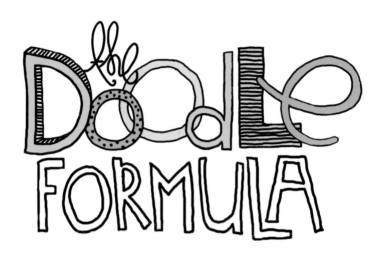

THE DOODLE FORMULA

ADRIENNE LOOMAN

Bluegrass Publishing

www.bluegrasspublishing.com

I REMEMBER

the day I chose to excel in drawing I was eight-years-old and going to an after school program. On this particular day, all the kids were gathered around a boy who was drawing. Curious about all the commotion, I asked, "What's going on?" My friend explained that this boy was drawing cool dolphins for everyone. Amazed at the response of the other kids to his work, I set out on a mission to draw better. I am convinced that my decision that day shaped me into who I am today. From that day forward, I drew everything and challenged myself each time the sun rose. Eventually, after years of drawing, I took a particular liking to doodling. Doodling is defined as "scribbling aimlessly," and I thought that was the best form of drawing because it allowed me to free my imagination instead of hindering it with restrictions. To doodle is to put on paper what you are feeling or thinking, and no one can critique that.

There have been countless times when a family member or friend asked, "How did you do that?" (referring to a drawing), and until now, I was always at a loss for words. See, every time people saw my drawings they would simply define my art as "talent," so naturally, after all those years, I began to think it was talent too—talent that no one else could reproduce. Then one glorious day, I was struck with a great realization! I began to notice a pattern in every one of my doodles. The excitement of this discovery was unbearable. I felt as though I had found "the key" everyone had been searching for.

Today, I beg to differ with those who claim drawing is a talent. Rather, my theory is that my determination at eight-years-old to be the best drawer anyone had ever seen and eighteen years of continued learning and striving is why I can draw the way I do… not because of sheer talent. If talent is simply something you are born with, then hypothetically speaking, a person born with the talent to swim could instantaneously win an Olympic gold medal without any formal training. But this doesn't happen. Instead, I believe that with dedication, proper training, and time, anyone can do anything—even draw.

The formula that you are about to learn is the pattern that I discovered in all my doodles. You will quickly learn that you don't need a steady hand, an eye for balance, or even talent to draw well.

I hope that after reading this book you will feel comfortable enough to release the most imaginative and creative side of yourself through drawing and incorporating doodling into everyday life.

Hugs, ADRIENNE

TABLE →of→ CONTENTS

Here's a quick reference guide to get you started on the chapters ahead.

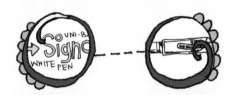
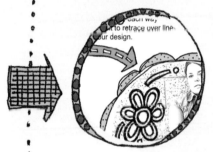
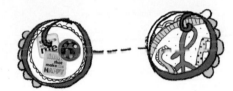

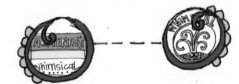

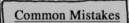
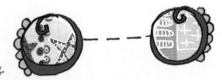

UTENSILS

PRO VS CON

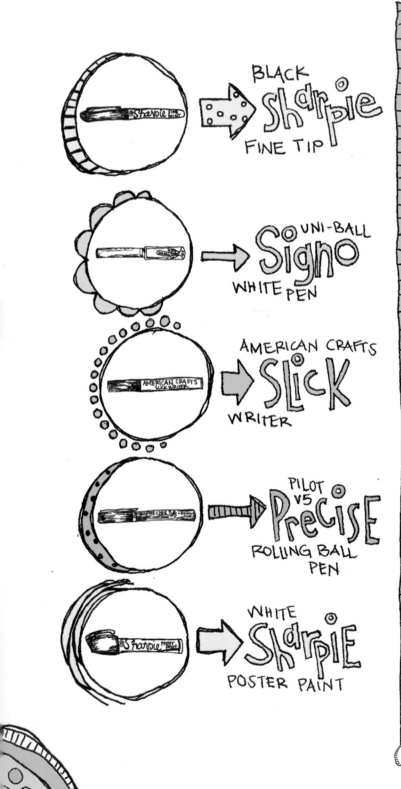

BLACK **Sharpie** FINE TIP

UNI-BALL **Signo** WHITE PEN

AMERICAN CRAFTS **Slick** WRITER

PILOT V5 **PreCise** ROLLING BALL PEN

WHITE **Sharpie** POSTER PAINT

Pro: This is my personal favorite. The tip size is versatile, and because it's permanent, it can write on any surface without smudging. Dries quickly and lasts a long time.

Con: If used on transparent materials such as glass, the color may appear more brown than black. Additionally, it has a tendancy to bleed on pourous materials. Not acid-free.

Pro: The Uni-Ball Signo has dominated the white pen market for some time now. Unlike other pens, Uni-Ball's ink does not skip and runs smooth. The white ink is very bright on dark surfaces and can be used on virtually any material. Acid-free.

Con: The pen does not last very long because the ink runs out quickly. Very difficult to find.

Pro: The Slick Writer specializes in writing on slick surfaces, such as photos or shiny objects and is permanent. Several tip sizes to choose from and, unlike the Sharpie, will look black on transparent materials. Acid-free.

Con: Similar to the Sharpie, this pen tends to bleed on pourus surfaces.

Pro: A necessity in my home, the Pilot V5 Precise pen offers an extremely tiny tip size, which is unique on the market. Ink runs smoothly, does not skip, and produces no bleeding on pourous surfaces like cardstock. A definite consideration if you are looking for a pen to create very detailed doodles.

Con: The V5 is not permanent, so it's limited to use on paper products. Acid status unknown.

Pro: The white Sharpie Poster Paint pen has several similarities to the Signo: it produces a bright white on dark surfaces and does not skip. This pen is permanent, so it may be used on any material and dries relatively quickly. I would have to say that, in my opinion and personal experience with several brands of white pens, this is the second best on the market.

Con: The fine tip on this pen is larger than other fine tips on the market. Requires shaking before each use.

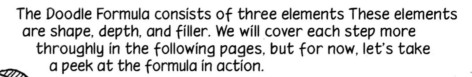

The Doodle Formula consists of three elements These elements are shape, depth, and filler. We will cover each step more throughly in the following pages, but for now, let's take a peek at the formula in action.

A shape is the most crucial part of this formula. Without a shape you have nothing to work off of. A shape does not have to be something you drew. Instead, it can be a design in patterned paper, an object in a photo, or simply a shaped embellishment.

Depth is the next step. Giving depth to your doodles makes them more pleasing to the eye and adds dimension to your drawing.

Finally, there are fillers. Fillers go hand-in-hand with depth. You fill the empty space around where you added depth with a filler. Fillers can consist of anything from a solid color to a pattern of dots.

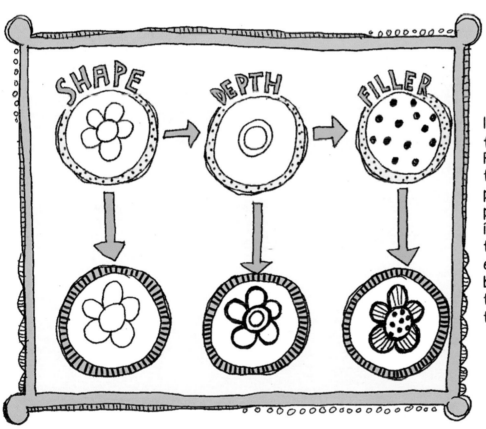

In this example I chose a flower shape to begin with. For depth, I retraced around the center and edges of the petals. Then for the filler, I put dots in the center, lines in the petals, and filled the tracings I did around the entire shape with a solid black. The end result is a thicker more unique flower than what I started out with.

Again, I will mention that you don't need a steady hand to create great doodles. It may be a good idea, however, to pay attention to the balance of your drawings. For example, if you freehand a straight line it may end up looking slanted. Statistics have shown that the human eye is attracted to symmetry. Therefore, I thought it might be helpful to include a section on ...

BaLANCE

When I say the human eye is attracted to symmetry, what I mean is that when we first focus on something our brain (unconsciously) dissects the image into pieces, which later help it form an understanding of what it just saw. This is easier and faster to do when things are balanced, thus quickly registering in your brain as something attractive. Unbalanced things (in general) are very hard for our brains to dissect and register quickly and ultimately may look unattractive to us.

Once you take the Doodle Personality Test (on p. 17), you might start wondering, "But Adrienne, if I have a messy doodle personality does that mean that the human eye will not be attracted to my artwork?" This is a little tricky. My answer would have to be "Yes and no." If you are a "messy" doodler and incorporate a sense of balance into your work, it will still be messy but attract the eye. If there is absolutely no sense of balance to your drawings, it's quite possible that your artwork will be less attractive.

Many people (I'm one of them) can read text all day long and never understand what they have read until they see it or do it for themselves. I've gone ahead and included several examples of how a balanced and messy doodler would draw the same shape. A balanced doodler relies on rulers and precise measurements, while a messy doodler would prefer to freehand and trash the ruler. Let's use borders as an example. Say you want to draw a border around your scrapbook layout. If you freehand this it may end up very unbalanced.

balanced circles

unbalanced circles

So, what I suggest is getting that ruler out and drawing the border with a pencil and ruler very lightly. This way you have an outline of a balanced border. Just because it's straight doesn't mean you must trace over it perfectly. In fact, just use the pencil line as a guide so that your lines do not slant off the page. For balanced circles, you can simply use a compass or you can trace around an object with a round, flat surface (like a glass or a penny) with a pencil. The penciled circle is just a guide. Be yourself—be messy if that is what is natural!

Using a pencil and a ruler, lightly draw a balanced line.

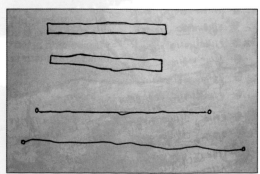

Then retrace that line with your pen, but you don't necessarily need to follow the line exactly. Think of this pencil line merely as a guide.

The top doodles in each of these pairs are messy, but they were created with a ruler, so they still please the eye. The bottom doodles in the examples were created without a ruler and are unbalanced—their messiness appears to be accidental instead of stylistic.

SHAPES

Before you do anything you must begin with a shape. This is the first step in the formula and also the most crucial. Without it you would have nothing to embellish.

This is also typically the hardest step for most people. A more experienced artist might be able to draw a really unique heart shape and others would consider that talent... but remember, I don't believe in talent (wink). Instead, I believe in practice and dedication. There is no easy path to drawing, and unfortunately, the skill doesn't come overnight.

However, with the right guidance, it is possible to excel at doodling more quickly than if you tried it on your own. Think of it as playing the guitar. If you just pick up a guitar one day and have never had lessons, it may take you years to figure out how to use it. Whereas, if you sought lessons from a guitar teacher, it may only take you a couple months.

There are several ways to obtain a shape for your first step. Traditionally, you could just draw one, but let's not restrict ourselves to one method. Try using the shape of an emellishment, or the designs in patterned paper. A cool thing I enjoy doing is an image search online because sometimes I want to draw a crown, but I'm not sure where to begin. Doing this kind of search brings me to a page full of photographed crowns, which I can print and then trace. Along the same line, if you want to draw a dog or a birthday cake you can look through your picture stash and simply trace one from your pictures.

Don't worry too much about having perfect drawings. As you can see from many of the doodles in this book, you don't necessarily need perfectly even shapes to produce a nice drawing.

Check out some of the examples below, illustrating different ways to obtain a base shape. When you are just starting out, it's a good idea to experiment with different techniques to find what interests you the most. Remember that you can also use hand drawn shapes, and if you get lost, try doing the image search online that I discuss.

You could use the letters in these chipboard pieces as your base shape.

In this example you could use the shape of the item or the design inside of it as your base shape.

Chipboard pieces are really great items to use. I love using chipboard swirls as my shape.

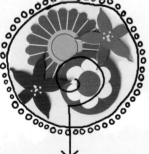

Don't forget about your stash of chipboard letters. Here you could use the letter, or the space inside.

These punch-out pieces are cool because I can use the petals, the center, or both as my base shape.

Try using button shapes, plastic flowers, or brads. These are just a few ideas to get you started.

Urban Lily chipboard circles, punch-out flowers, Queen and Company Fontastics, Fab Flowers, KI Memories, Making Memories puffy flower, Bazzill brads, Rouge De Garance punch-outs, generic buttons.

Below is an example of several different patterned papers. I drew dotted lines around parts of the designs which would be great to use as a shape. I would suggest, if you choose a complicated design, using only a portion of it, so your finished design is not too "busy."

Rouge De Garance, KI Memories, Hambly Screenprints, A2Z essentials, Scrap in Style TV, Bam Pop, Sassafras Lass, Cherry Arte.

"Girlbot"
artwork created by
James A. Demski Jr.
www.jimbot.com
jim@jimbot.com
Used with permission from the artist

Earlier I mentioned that you could obtain a shape by tracing a piece of artwork or picture. If you look to the left you will see "Girlbot," a piece of art I admire by the artist "Jimbot." I wanted to re-create the outline of the robot for my shape. I started by printing it out. Then I laid a sheet of polyurethane on top and traced along the edges. All I wanted was to get the basic shape of the character so that I could move on to the other parts of the formula. Once I completed that, I seperated the two sheets and threw the original print-out away.

You should recognize the spirals on the right side of this layout from the American Crafts paper design on the previous page. When I see a piece of patterned paper, my mind instantly begins to think of what I can use as a shape to base my doodles on. The funky shape on the bottom of this layout was based off of a flower patterned paper by American Crafts. Flowers work really well because they allow me to implement the formula in a lot of different ways and they are typically big enough for me to get really creative. If I choose a very small design, such as a tiny butterfly, I may not have a lot of room to doodle. Every design in patterned paper has some element that can be altered through doodling. I encourage you to start looking through your paper stash and challenging yourself to find at least two or three elements on each sheet that you can use for shapes.

Use the design in patterned paper as your shape.

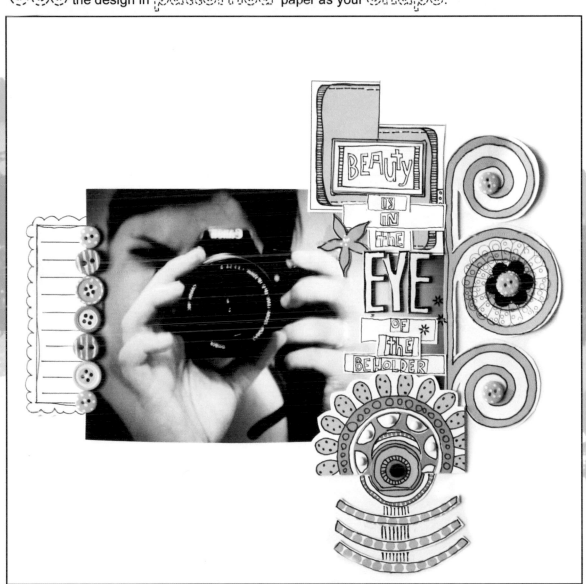

Patterned paper: American Crafts, Rouge De Garance, Urban Lily. Letters: Heidi Swapp. Rub-ons: Urban Lily. Pilot Precise V5 ink pen.

With embellishments often your shapes have already been created for you. For instance, if you are using a chipboard alphabet, you won't have to look for a design because the letter will be your shape. Some chipboard alphabets have polka dot designs on them, so you could also use the polka dots as your shapes and continue to use the formula on those.

The shape for the green box on the top of the layout is from Urban Lily's box paper. I just cut out the box, doodled on it, and then cut it in half and displaced it a little.

Depth plays an important role in any design. It can make your image look fancy, playful, serious, or whimsical, depending on how much of it you incorporate into your drawing. There are two ways you can add depth. The first way is to outline all or part of your design and the second way is to retrace the lines of the design. In the example below, I used both ways of creating depth.

Outlining the design makes the image look thick and three dimensional. Retracing the lines makes the design seem more intense.

I encourage you to experiment with this step in the formula and try different variations of each way to include depth. You may want to trace over lines in a loose, messy manner or only outline half of your design.

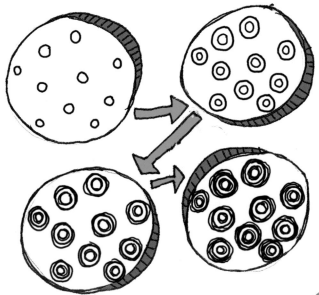

In the example to the left, I began with the simple shape of a circle. Watch as I outline the circle and then include several layers of depth by retracing the lines. I used a messy technique for retracing in this example, but you can also try to retrace your lines more precisely, which produces a different effect.

Only you can determine how many layers of depth are necessary for your project. Experimenting will be your best tool for discovering your favorite method.

Depth: (depth) n. 1. The distance from the top downward, or from front to back. 2. Deepness. 3. Intensity. 4. The deepest or inmost part.

What better way for you to test your new depth knowledge than to use it in a drawing? Go ahead and add different kinds of depth to the doodles below. You may even want to make photocopies of this page so that you can try a different way on each copy and then lay them all out together and decide which kinds of depth you like best. Keep in mind that you can trace over the lines as a way to add depth.

In addition to the experimenting you will do with the shapes I've given you on this page, you may enjoy exploring this step on your own. Above I've shown an example of a piece of paper that originally was decorated with a bunch of very plain flowers. I had a lot of fun adding depth to the different aspects of the flowers.

Try to remember that you don't necessarily need to include depth in every single design, but maybe only in a few petals on a flower, or possibly the flower center, keeping the petals plain. By experimenting, you gain knowledge of the doodling process, a feel for what you like best, and some new designs that you can use on future projects.

Patterned paper: Rouge De Garance (series limited), Scrap in Style TV. Kelli Crowe flowers. Letters: Queen and Company. Embellishments: Lil' Davis Designs, Doodlebug.

Adding depth to this layout was pretty simple. I retraced the flower centers and the checker circles on the left. Notice that I used a white pen on the brown, blue, and green (such as the chipboard letters and the blue "blades" at the bottom of the page). This contrast really adds to the shapes' depth. I also traced around the white marks with black on occasion to make particular designs pop from the page. I really wanted the brown and blue doodled flowers to be more noticeable, but if I had traced along them in black, it would have done nothing because the colors are already dark (more about this in "Common Mistakes"). With the white outlines, the flowers really stand out and they have more color and depth.

Also, using lighter doodles on top and darker doodles on bottom of the layout tells the viewer to focus first on the picture of my aunt.

So far we have covered two of the three parts to the formula. We learned that you start with a shape and then add depth. The third and last part to the formula is what I like to call a "filler." This step is actually my favorite. It's the part where you can start including fun embellishments in your design. Think of a filler as a paint bucket, except instead of solid colors, you have patterns.

As you may gather from the examples below, a filler is usually a mixture, of repetitive patterns. You can use these patterns in any "white space" that is left from the design you have created. As an example, you can see that I used a tiny stripe filler inside the scallops that frame the title of this page.

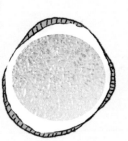  

To the left you can see several examples that I have included to help you out, but I really would like to encourage you to keep a small journal of filler ideas as well. There are innumerable possibilities when looking for fillers. Above you will see three pictures. The first one I took of the sliding glass on one of my bathroom cabinets. The second is bark from a tree. The third is a rug in my home. I've included these pictures to show that everywhere you look you can find inspiration to create your very own fillers, so that you are not stuck using polka dots all the time.

A method that you may want to try is to take a picture of something you think would look cool as a filler. Then if you have the capabilities to do so, open your photo in your image design program and in the channels or color adjustment settings, change the photo to grayscale. From there, open the contrast tool, setting it full blast. This will make anything that is dark grey, black and anything that is light grey, white. The picture will then look like an ink drawing and will give you a better idea of how that particular design would look if used as a filler.

There are several ways to implement this step of the formula, but I almost always use a filler in the depth that I created. For example, if I used a circle shape and added depth by tracing a larger circle around the base shape, I almost always will put a filler between those two circles.

Now that you have seen some of my filler ideas, it's time for you to explore as well. There are several ways to gather inspiration for a filler, such as logos, tile desgins, the natural environment (wood, for example), architecture, etc. Almost anything you look at can be turned into a filler, so use the empty spaces below to add some of your own fillers based on what you see around you. Later, when you are doodling and it comes time to implement this step, you can just flip to this page and use a filler that you've drawn.

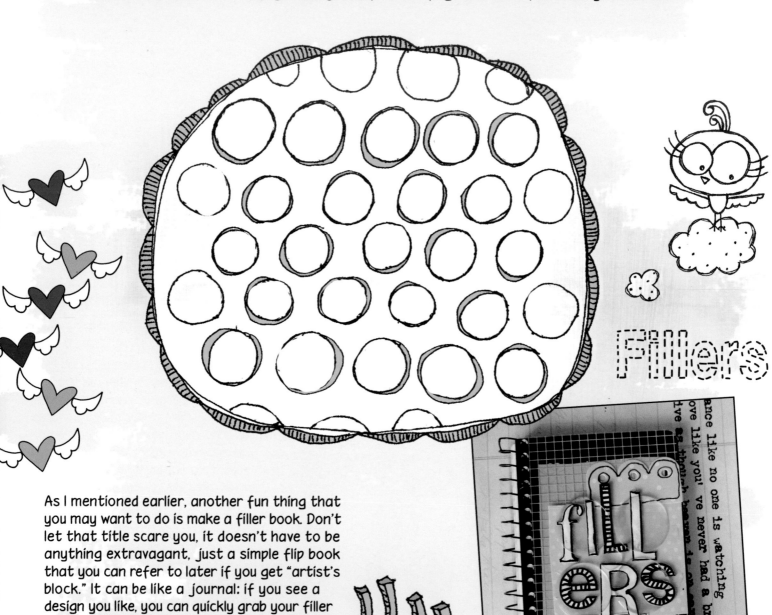

Fillers

As I mentioned earlier, another fun thing that you may want to do is make a filler book. Don't let that title scare you, it doesn't have to be anything extravagant, just a simple flip book that you can refer to later if you get "artist's block." It can be like a journal: if you see a design you like, you can quickly grab your filler book and jot it down. Or keep your filler book by your bed, and if you saw something earlier that day that would make a great filler, you can add it into your book before you snooze. Keep in mind that if any of your friends are learning the Doodle Formula as well, you can exchange your filler ideas. Having a filler book is a great way to keep your (and your friends') ideas fresh. If you glance over to the right, you can see an example of my filler book.

Try **using** the **formula** straight on your **pictures**.

What if I said that you can use something in your photo as a shape? I wanted to cover up the distracting background in this photo, so I outlined our heads to give myself an idea of my shape. I only kept our faces away from the filler. I used a loose filler, scribbling back and forth across the background, blocking out the distractions without making the filler too dark. Then I added depth by retracing parts of our faces, such as our eyebrows and eyelashes. You'll notice that I also used a circle filler in the lower right-hand corner of the layout and a stripe filler on the bottom border of the photo.

Patterned paper: Hambly Screenprints, Bam Pop. Letters: Doodlebug. Other supplies: buttons.

Now that we have covered the formula, let's dig a little deeper and discover your doodle personality! Learning more about yourself will help improve your doodling skills. In my opinion, there are three kinds of doodle styles: intricate, whimsical, and cartoon. Below you will see the differences between them.

An intricate doodler focuses on complex details and is usually best at doodling exactly what the image would look like in real life (i.e. the intricate doodler would draw a flower, and when the doodle was finished, it would be very fancy and life-like).

A whimsical doodler focuses on exaggeration in drawings. A flower may have normal sized petals but huge leaves. The drawing may include fancy details, but the exaggerations keep the image from looking as life-like as the intricate doodler's.

my choice	AdriENNE's
Favorite Style	Favorite Style
Cartoon	Whimsical
Favorite Form	Favorite Form
Messy	Messy
Natural Style	Natural Style
whimsical	whimsical
Natural Form	Natural Form
Messy	Messy

Lastly, a cartoon doodler is a mix of the others, except highly exaggerated (more than the whimsical doodler). A cartoon doodler's drawings can include extreme detail work but will rarely look life-like and are typically very puffy in nature with few hard edges.

To the left are examples of the three styles. Go ahead and choose which one you like best. When you've made your choice, write it in the box above. I've added mine already.

Now I want you to check out the two other styles: "balanced" and "messy." A balanced doodler tends to draw symetrically, whereas a messy one will be more asymetrical.

Again, once you have made your choice, write it in the box above.

YouR doodle PERSonality...

Now that we have our favorites, I'll bet you're thinking this is your doodle personality, but surprise!! It's not. Actually, your doodle personality refers to the style that you are best at. Some people may be extraordinarily intricate doodlers. Their whole lives they might try to be whimsical, thus keeping themselves from a style that they had incredible potential for. Now, you might be thinking to yourself, "But Adrienne, if you don't believe in talent, how can you claim that I am magically better at one style than the next?" It's true. I don't believe in talent; I believe in intense practice. I see your natural style as the doodle personality you have developed, and just as your personality develops, so will your doodles. Have I confused you? An example is your signature. Some people have cartoonish signatures, while others have signatures with well defined letters.

Growing up, you may have unknowingly practiced a particular style enough to excel in that area but lack ability in others. Now I want you to look over the examples again and imagine yourself drawing each design in all 3 styles. You will need to decide which one you think you, honestly, would be the best at. Some of you may get lucky and draw best in the style that is your favorite, but others, unfortunately, will have to choose styles other than their favorites. Once you have made your decision, go ahead and write that down in the box on the left.

Congratulations! You have just figured out your doodle personality! Of course, just because you have one style does not mean that you have to use that style forever. I would suggest that you at least get acquainted with your personality and really try to excel at it. After all, this is what you are naturally inclined to draw. However, you can do anything with enough practice. I'm sure you have heard that things like this "don't happen overnight." It's true. You will be trying to change your natural doodle personality, so understandably, it will take a long time and lots of practice. But believe me, it is possible.

COMMON MISTAKES

Even though I generally do not put restrictions on myself when I draw, I will admit that there are some things I avoid. This is not because these things are wrong, but to me, these things are not visually pleasing or they appear overwhelming. I have catagorized these ideas as "dos and don'ts" and have included some examples below.

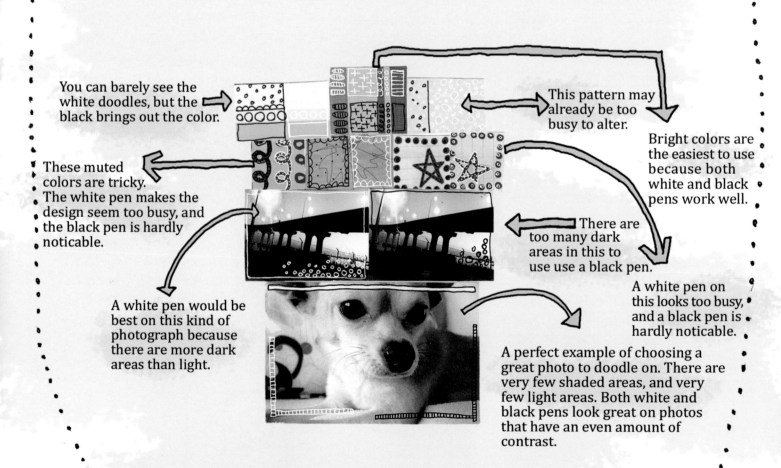

You can barely see the white doodles, but the black brings out the color.

This pattern may already be too busy to alter.

These muted colors are tricky. The white pen makes the design seem too busy, and the black pen is hardly noticable.

Bright colors are the easiest to use because both white and black pens work well.

There are too many dark areas in this to use use a black pen.

A white pen would be best on this kind of photograph because there are more dark areas than light.

A white pen on this looks too busy, and a black pen is hardly noticable.

A perfect example of choosing a great photo to doodle on. There are very few shaded areas, and very few light areas. Both white and black pens look great on photos that have an even amount of contrast.

Experiment with various colors.

Keeping in mind the information from the Common Mistakes lesson,
I completed a layout using muted colors such as kraft and dark brown.
Here you may notice I used the dark on light method.

Patterned paper: Urban Lily, Hambly Screenprints, Love, Elsie, Rouge De Garance.
Letters: Heidi Swapp. Rub-ons: Urban Lily. Embellishments: Prima, 7 Gypsies, Autumn Leaves.

SCRAPBOOKING IdEAS
and projects

its like

cloud9

Hello

Now that you have seen and learned the formula, let's look at several ways to incorporate doodling into your own projects.

One of my favorite things to do is to doodle on my scrapbook pages. I feel that when I do this I am adding a more personal touch to them.

You will probably begin to notice that I use polka dots and stripes often. These are my favorite fillers, but I encourage you to experiment with others as well.

Patterned paper: Rouge De Garance.
Embellishments: Bazzill, Making Memories, Cloud 9 Designs, Queen and Company, Prima. Letters: Heidi Swapp.

Try making your own patterned paper by doodling random designs clustered together. You can even scan it into your computer and print several sheets.

In this layout I first created the paper you see to the left. I then cut a couple of my favorite flowers out and embellished them as you see in the final layout. I can also cut strips of the paper for future projects.

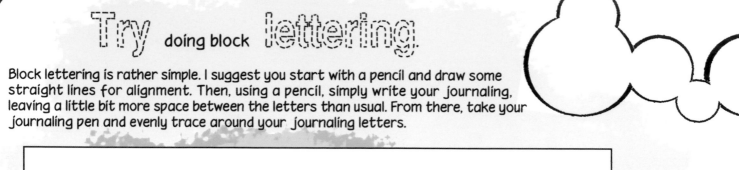

Try doing block lettering

Block lettering is rather simple. I suggest you start with a pencil and draw some straight lines for alignment. Then, using a pencil, simply write your journaling, leaving a little bit more space between the letters than usual. From there, take your journaling pen and evenly trace around your journaling letters.

Patterned paper: Scrap in Style TV, Doodlebug, Hambly Screenprints. Letters: Heidi Swapp. Rub-ons: Urban Lily. Other supplies: orange pen, buttons.

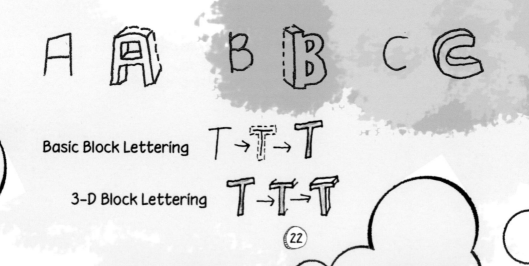

Basic Block Lettering T → T → T

3-D Block Lettering T → T → T

Borders

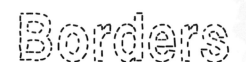

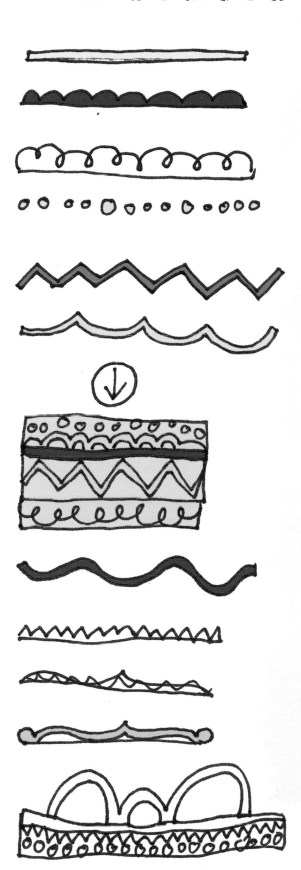

Here is just a sampling of the different kinds of borders you can use on your pages. You'll notice that some of the borders are actually combinations of several different styles. This can give your page a more ornate look. Sometimes, however, a more ornate border can detract from your photo. Before you add a border decide where you want your focus to be and what kind of look you want your page to have.

Below is a layout I created which illustrates the use of a variety of borders. This was a simple layout to create because some of the guess work was already done for me. Creative Imaginations' scalloped patterned paper already gave me the design I needed to start the formula. Did you happen to notice that only two borders and the chipboard letters have fillers? Remember, your filler is like a paint can of patterns, but it can also be blank or a solid color. Because I created very strong borders around the paper, I decided to keep the paper simple, thus creating balance.

Experiment with making your own borders like the ones here. Try circles, zigzags, hearts, flowers, scallops, etc.

Patterned paper: Creative Imaginations. Letters: Heidi Swapp. Embellishments: Doodlebug, Prima, Queen and Company, Bazzill.

In this layout, "It's Like Cloud 9," I wanted to make the entire page fit the cloud theme. A border with thick black lines can make a page seem heavy or rough, the opposite of light and fluffy. Here I used the same formula that I always use, but I changed my pen. Instead of a fine tip Sharpie, I used the Precise V5 pen, which draws smaller lines. Also, I was careful to maintain a sense of balance with the boxes and lines that I drew around the photo and for the journaling. Even though my lines are messy, they do not slant off the page. These borders are a perfect example of using pencil lines as guides for your pen.

The clouds and the scalloped paper help break up the black lines of the border on this page and give it a softer look. After cutting out the clouds from a piece of paper, I traced along them several times (adding depth) and left them blank in the middle, like real clouds (i.e. I used a blank filler). The scalloped paper already had white dots on it, so I retraced along the edges adding depth, I also added a smaller polka dot filler. Notice how my fillers were either blank or very subtle, matching the cloud theme.

Patterned paper: Rouge De Garance, Bam Pop, Creative Imaginations, Tinkering Ink, Hambly Screenprints overlay. Letters: Heidi Swapp. Rub-Ons: Urban Lily. Other supplies: buttons.

In this layout, I have used multiple layers of the formula. First, I began with a simple border around the photo. Then I added scallops on the left and right sides. I created depth by putting half circles inside the scallops. I added a stripe filler to the original shape that borders the picture.

I have piles of photos with very distracting backgrounds. This creates a dilemma because I hate cutting photos down. Take the photo in this layout for example: I wanted to keep the background because I want to remember all of the Christmas decorations in the house. But at the same time, I want to focus on the point of the picture: our toast. I created "blinds" by starting with a rectangle shape and then adding a stripe filler. Then I adhered white lollipop sticks to grab the eye and draw it toward the people in the picture instead of the background. Also notice that, although the border is fairly ornate, it is small enough that it does not detract from the photo.

Patterned paper: Rouge De Garance, Creative Imaginations, Urban Lily, Autumn Leaves. Letters: Heidi Swapp. Rub-ons: Urban Lily, Hambly Screenprints. Embellishments: Autumn Leaves, Bazzill, Heidi Swapp, Queen and Company. Other Supplies: miniature doily.

THIS IS JUST A few things you cAN Find IN DAVIDS UNCLE OFFICE

Patterned paper: Rouge De Garance. Embellishments: Doodlebug.

You may wonder what in the world an intensified swirl is. An intensified swirl is a swirl that is completely crammed with filler. To get a better idea, take a look at the layout above. Notice that on the top left and bottom right corners I have doodled a swirl shape and used an intensely detailed circle filler. These swirls balance the layout and add to its "wild" look.

Try drawing some kind of border of swirls and including very detailed fillers in your shapes. See the examples on either side of the layout above to get a better idea of what this may look like. One example is a blank swirl. The other two show how different types of filler give the swirl a more intense look.

Journaling

May I tell you a secret? Though you might never have guessed it, there was a time when I relied solely on my computer for fonts for journaling and titles that I could print out! This computer-dependence could be very tedious at times, but I didn't trust myself enough to journal directly on my pages.

At one point I was at a crop (an all day scrapbooking event) with my aunt and I couldn't complete my layouts because I didn't have a computer with me. I felt that I would ruin them if I tried to write on my layouts. Eventually I got frustrated and began to look at some of the rub-on alphabets I had. I remember spending around 3 hours copying the rub-ons' font. It wasn't perfect but good enough in my eyes.

Below I used the journaling strips method. In the title, I used black pen on white letters to create contrast. This also creates a stark look that goes with the idea of being afraid. However, to lighten the tone of the title up a little, I made the word *deathly* more whimsical, which contrasts with the harsher look of the chipboard letters in *afraid*.

Patterned paper: Urban Lily, Rouge De Garance, Hambly Screenprints overlay.
Letters: Heidi Swapp. Skull rub-on: Hambly Screenprints. Embellishments: Urban Lily
chipboard block, buttons, lace trim.

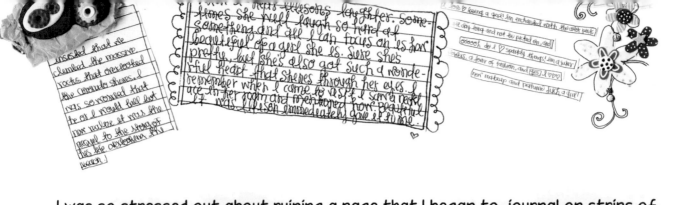

I was so stressed out about ruining a page that I began to journal on strips of paper so that if one word came out wrong I could just throw the strip away, instead of the whole layout. Strips of journaling also add a slightly 3-dimensional look to a page, so this may be a perfect method for those who are looking to break away from their dependency on computers.

Here's a tip! If you're a perfectionist, use your normal handwriting but write really tiny. When you do this it is hard for your brain to see or register any "mistakes."

In the layout below I created a "journaling box." I've added very light lines, so that my journaling will be balanced. For the title, I outlined the word *yes* to add depth, and I used polka dots on the *y* and the *s*, but not the *e*, to create contrast and to keep the layout from looking too busy. (Notice the *E* is capitalized, but the other letters are not. This also creates contrast and gives the page a fun look.)

Patterned paper: Scrap in Style TV, Rouge De Garance. Rub-ons: Rouge De Garance. Other supplies: "Sonora High" collection at Scrap in Style TV.

Alter things you typically throw away

This canister originally held foam flowers. Usually, once I have used the products inside these containers, I would throw the containers in the trash. Instead, I altered this container to use again as decoration or as storage for miscellaneous items in my scrapbooking area. I have illustrated the transformation below incorporating the Doodle Formula.

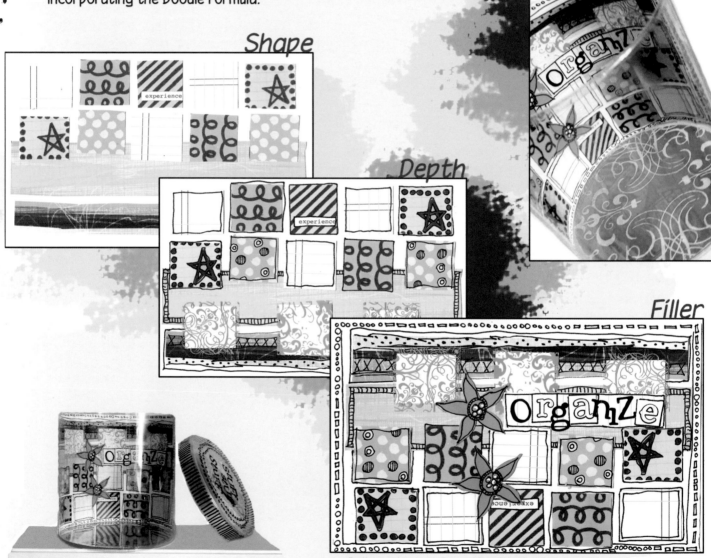

Shape

Depth

Filler

Patterned paper: Rouge De Garance, Love, Elsie. Transparencies: Hambly Screenprints. Letters: Doodlebug. Flowers: Rouge De Garance.

Ordinary Items —
Extraordinary Doodling

You know those frames you have? They too can be doodled on! Here are a few that I altered using the formula.

You can also use the formula to make great gifts for friends or children by doodling on a clipboard. This one in particular was somewhat transparent and flexible, which, after being doodled on, looks really unique.

Using paint pens and permanent markers you can alter just about anything! I even decorated some brightly colored acrylic drinking glasses to use as decoration in my room.

MY

BRUISER

Patterned paper: Rouge De Garance, Creative Imaginations, Hambly Screenprints, Urban Lily, Doodlebug, Scrap in Style TV. Letters: Doodlebug. Other supplies: glass pebbles, canvas, paint.

There are several fun ways to incorporate doodling in your life, such as this canvas wall art I made. For this project I punched out small circles and used them underneath my border of clear glass pebbles. The pebbles magnify the designs in the paper circles and give them a funky, 3-D look.

1. Adhere your picture to the canvas.

2. Paint along the edges of the photo, making sure to get some paint on the canvas as well (see the pink border).

3. While you're waiting for the paint to dry, use a circle punch to make the round pieces of patterned paper to go behind the pebbles. Pick a punch that makes circles slightly smaller than your glass pebbles. You can use leftover scraps from your favorite scrapbook paper, wallpaper, cardstock, etc. You can also doodle on your circles and the pebbles will magnify the doodles.

4. Adhere the paper circles around the edges of the canvas with a permanent glue runner or a hot glue gun.

5. Adhere the pebbles onto the paper circles using a hot glue gun.

6. Once the paint is dry add strips of Hambly around the edges of your photo and then outline them using a permanent marker.

7. Outline the outermost edge of the paint and add a filler to the middle (I used polka dots).

8. Outline the pebbles (if you want to).

9. Add your title.

10. Hang that baby on the wall!

"What better way to leave a legacy
than to utilize your imagination through the tip of a pen?"

~ *Adrienne Looman*